EMMANUEL JOSEPH

The Digital Colosseum, Where Sports, AI, and Mythological Heroes Collide

Copyright © 2025 by Emmanuel Joseph

All rights reserved. No part of this publication may be reproduced, stored or transmitted in any form or by any means, electronic, mechanical, photocopying, recording, scanning, or otherwise without written permission from the publisher. It is illegal to copy this book, post it to a website, or distribute it by any other means without permission.

First edition

This book was professionally typeset on Reedsy.
Find out more at reedsy.com

Contents

1	Chapter 1: The Dawn of the Digital Colosseum	1
2	Chapter 2: The Legacy of Heroes	3
3	Chapter 3: The Architects of Athlon	5
4	Chapter 4: Trials and Triumphs	7
5	Chapter 5: The Art of Adaptation	9
6	Chapter 6: Bonds of Brotherhood	11
7	Chapter 7: The Edge of Innovation	13
8	Chapter 8: The Champions' Circle	15
9	Chapter 9: The Aftermath of Victory	17
10	Chapter 10: Legends Reborn	19
11	Chapter 11: The Evolution of Athlon	21
12	Chapter 12: A New Dawn	23
13	Chapter 13: The Rise of New Legends	25
14	Chapter 14: The Global Impact	27
15	Chapter 15: The Future Awaits	29

1

Chapter 1: The Dawn of the Digital Colosseum

In a future where technology reigns supreme, the landscape of sports has evolved beyond recognition. Virtual arenas have replaced traditional stadiums, and spectators from around the globe now gather in a vast digital space to witness the ultimate display of athletic prowess. The Digital Colosseum stands as a testament to this new era, a sprawling virtual coliseum where athletes and mythological heroes alike compete in breathtaking, high-stakes battles.

At the heart of the Digital Colosseum lies the AI Engine, a powerful artificial intelligence that governs the events and ensures a fair and thrilling competition. This AI, named Athlon, has been designed to simulate the abilities of legendary heroes and ancient gods, bringing them to life in the virtual realm. Athlon's creation marks the beginning of a new age, where the lines between reality and fantasy blur, and the spirit of competition reaches unprecedented heights.

As the Digital Colosseum's inaugural event approaches, the world eagerly anticipates the clash of titans. Athletes from all corners of the globe have trained tirelessly to compete, honing their skills and pushing the boundaries of human potential. The arena is abuzz with excitement, as fans prepare to witness history in the making. The Digital Colosseum promises to be a spectacle unlike any other, a celebration of human ingenuity and the timeless allure of competition.

Among the contenders is Alex, a rising star in the world of digital sports. Driven by a desire to prove himself and achieve greatness, Alex has dedicated his life to mastering the art of combat within the Digital Colosseum. As he steps into the virtual arena for the first time, he feels the weight of expectation on his shoulders. The eyes of the world are upon him, and the stage is set for an epic confrontation that will test his limits and redefine the future of sports.

2

Chapter 2: The Legacy of Heroes

As the crowd in the Digital Colosseum swells with anticipation, the stories of the legendary heroes come to life, woven into the fabric of the competition. These mythological figures have been meticulously recreated by Athlon, their abilities and characteristics faithfully mirrored in the virtual world. The likes of Achilles, Hercules, and Athena now stride the digital battlefield, their presence a testament to the enduring power of myth and legend.

Each hero brings with them a unique set of skills and attributes, carefully balanced to ensure an exhilarating contest. Achilles, with his unparalleled speed and invulnerability, stands as a fearsome opponent, while Hercules' raw strength and resilience make him a force to be reckoned with. Athena's strategic brilliance and wisdom lend her a distinct edge, as she outmaneuvers and outthinks her rivals. The stage is set for an epic showdown, where the boundaries between myth and reality blur in the heat of battle.

The athletes who enter the Digital Colosseum must not only contend with their human competitors but also face the might of these legendary figures. The challenge is immense, as they strive to match the prowess of heroes who have been immortalized in stories for centuries. Yet, it is this very challenge that drives them, pushing them to reach new heights and achieve feats that were once thought impossible.

As the first round of the competition begins, the crowd watches in awe as athletes and heroes clash in a dazzling display of skill and determination. Each battle is a testament to the power of the human spirit, as the athletes draw inspiration from the legends of old and strive to carve out their own place in history. The Digital Colosseum becomes a crucible of dreams and ambitions, where the past and the future converge in a spectacular fusion of athleticism and myth.

3

Chapter 3: The Architects of Athlon

The creation of Athlon, the AI Engine powering the Digital Colosseum, was a monumental achievement, brought to life by a team of brilliant scientists and engineers. Led by Dr. Elena Carter, a visionary in the field of artificial intelligence, the team worked tirelessly to develop an AI capable of simulating the abilities of mythological heroes and ensuring a fair and dynamic competition. Their efforts culminated in the birth of Athlon, a groundbreaking fusion of technology and imagination.

Dr. Carter's journey began with a simple yet ambitious idea: to create an AI that could bring the legends of the past to life in a virtual arena. Drawing inspiration from her childhood fascination with mythology and her passion for cutting-edge technology, she assembled a diverse team of experts, each contributing their unique skills and perspectives to the project. Together, they navigated the challenges of developing an AI that could adapt to the unpredictable nature of competitive sports while maintaining the integrity of ancient myths.

Athlon's development was a painstaking process, requiring countless hours of coding, testing, and refinement. The team meticulously studied the legends of heroes like Achilles, Hercules, and Athena, translating their abilities into algorithms and ensuring that each hero's characteristics were faithfully represented in the virtual world. The result was an AI that could not only simulate the strengths and weaknesses of these legendary figures but also evolve and learn from each competition, constantly improving and adapting to new challenges.

As the launch of the Digital Colosseum approached, Dr. Carter and her team faced one final hurdle: ensuring that Athlon would be accepted by the global community of athletes and fans. They organized a series of demonstration events, showcasing the AI's capabilities and the thrilling potential of the virtual arena. The response was overwhelmingly positive, with athletes eager to test their skills against the legendary heroes and fans captivated by the spectacle. With the stage set and the world watching, the Digital Colosseum was poised to revolutionize the world of sports and entertainment.

4

Chapter 4: Trials and Triumphs

As the competition in the Digital Colosseum progresses, athletes face a series of grueling trials designed to test their limits and push them to new heights. Each round brings new challenges, with the AI-controlled mythological heroes presenting formidable obstacles. The athletes must adapt quickly, leveraging their unique strengths and strategies to overcome their legendary opponents and advance to the next stage of the tournament.

Alex, the rising star, finds himself pitted against Hercules in a battle of strength and endurance. The virtual arena transforms into a landscape of ancient ruins, where the two combatants engage in a fierce struggle. Hercules' raw power and resilience are daunting, but Alex's agility and resourcefulness give him an edge. As the battle rages on, Alex draws on his training and determination, refusing to yield to the overwhelming force of his opponent. In a climactic moment, he manages to outmaneuver Hercules, securing a hard-fought victory and earning the admiration of the crowd.

Throughout the competition, the athletes form bonds of camaraderie and mutual respect, united by their shared experiences and the trials they face. They exchange tips and strategies, learning from each other's strengths and weaknesses. The Digital Colosseum becomes a melting pot of cultures and backgrounds, where athletes from different corners of the world come together to celebrate the spirit of competition and the pursuit of excellence.

THE DIGITAL COLOSSEUM, WHERE SPORTS, AI, AND MYTHOLOGICAL HEROES COLLIDE

As the tournament progresses, the stakes grow higher, and the challenges become more intense. The athletes must dig deep, summoning every ounce of their skill and determination to prevail. Each victory brings them one step closer to the ultimate prize: the title of Digital Champion, a symbol of their triumph over both human and mythological adversaries. The journey is arduous, but the promise of glory drives them forward, spurring them to achieve feats that will be remembered for generations to come.

5

Chapter 5: The Art of Adaptation

As the competition intensifies, the athletes must adapt to an ever-changing array of challenges and environments. The Digital Colosseum's AI Engine, Athlon, continuously generates new scenarios, each more complex and demanding than the last. From ancient battlefields to futuristic landscapes, the virtual arenas push the athletes to their limits, testing their creativity, resilience, and ability to think on their feet.

One such challenge sees Alex and his fellow competitors transported to a virtual rendition of Mount Olympus. Here, they must navigate treacherous terrain and overcome mythical creatures, all while contending with the formidable presence of the gods themselves. Alex finds himself pitted against Athena, the goddess of wisdom and warfare. Her strategic brilliance and unparalleled combat skills make her a daunting opponent, but Alex remains undeterred.

Drawing on his experiences and the lessons learned from previous battles, Alex devises a plan to outwit Athena. He leverages the environment to his advantage, using the rocky terrain and ancient ruins to create traps and ambushes. The battle is fierce and grueling, but Alex's determination and adaptability shine through. In a climactic showdown, he manages to outmaneuver the goddess, securing another hard-fought victory and earning the respect of his peers.

The Digital Colosseum becomes a crucible of innovation and ingenuity, as athletes constantly evolve and refine their strategies to stay ahead of the competition. They learn to harness the unique properties of each virtual arena, turning obstacles into opportunities and exploiting the weaknesses of their opponents. The spirit of adaptation and perseverance becomes a defining characteristic of the tournament, as the athletes push the boundaries of what is possible in the digital realm.

6

Chapter 6: Bonds of Brotherhood

Amidst the fierce competition, the athletes form deep and lasting bonds with one another. The shared experiences and challenges they face create a sense of camaraderie and mutual respect, transcending the boundaries of nationality and background. The Digital Colosseum becomes a melting pot of cultures and ideas, where athletes from all walks of life come together to celebrate the spirit of competition and the pursuit of excellence.

Alex finds himself forging friendships with athletes from diverse corners of the globe. They share stories of their journeys, their struggles, and their dreams, finding common ground in their shared passion for the sport. These bonds of brotherhood become a source of strength and support, as the athletes encourage and inspire one another to reach new heights. In the face of adversity, they stand united, knowing that their collective spirit and determination can overcome any obstacle.

The friendships formed within the Digital Colosseum extend beyond the virtual arena, influencing the athletes' lives in profound and meaningful ways. They exchange tips and strategies, learn from each other's strengths and weaknesses, and celebrate each other's successes. The sense of community and camaraderie becomes a defining aspect of the tournament, as the athletes push themselves to achieve feats that will be remembered for generations to come.

As the competition progresses, the bonds of brotherhood are tested by the relentless pressure and intensity of the challenges. Yet, it is this very pressure that strengthens their resolve and deepens their connections. The athletes draw on the support and encouragement of their peers, finding the courage to face their fears and overcome their doubts. In the end, it is the bonds of brotherhood that propel them to greatness, as they strive to etch their names into the annals of history.

7

Chapter 7: The Edge of Innovation

Innovation becomes the driving force behind the competition in the Digital Colosseum. The athletes and their teams constantly seek new ways to gain an edge, experimenting with cutting-edge technology and creative strategies. The integration of AI, virtual reality, and advanced training techniques pushes the boundaries of what is possible, transforming the way athletes prepare for and compete in the tournament.

Alex and his team embrace this spirit of innovation, utilizing state-of-the-art training facilities and simulations to refine their skills. They study the movements and techniques of their opponents, using AI-driven analytics to identify patterns and weaknesses. This data-driven approach allows them to fine-tune their strategies and develop unique tactics tailored to each challenge they face. The relentless pursuit of innovation becomes a cornerstone of their success, propelling them to new heights in the Digital Colosseum.

The virtual arenas themselves are a testament to the power of innovation, each one meticulously designed to provide a unique and immersive experience. From ancient temples to futuristic cities, the environments challenge the athletes to adapt and excel in diverse settings. The Digital Colosseum becomes a showcase of human ingenuity and creativity, where the fusion of technology and imagination brings the world of sports to life in breathtaking ways.

As the competition progresses, the athletes continue to push the envelope, exploring new techniques and strategies to stay ahead of their rivals. The spirit of innovation becomes a defining characteristic of the tournament, inspiring a new generation of athletes to dream big and embrace the possibilities of the digital age. The Digital Colosseum stands as a testament to the power of human creativity and the endless potential of technological advancement.

8

Chapter 8: The Champions' Circle

As the tournament reaches its climax, the field of competitors narrows, and the remaining athletes prepare for the final, most challenging rounds. The stakes are higher than ever, with the title of Digital Champion and the accompanying glory within reach. The athletes' journey to this point has been arduous, filled with trials and triumphs, but they remain resolute in their pursuit of greatness.

The final rounds bring together the best of the best, showcasing the incredible skill, determination, and resilience of the top contenders. The battles are fierce and closely contested, with each athlete giving their all to secure victory. The virtual arenas are filled with the roar of the crowd, as fans from around the world tune in to witness the crowning of the Digital Champion.

Alex finds himself among the elite, his journey marked by hard-fought victories and moments of brilliance. As he prepares for the final showdown, he reflects on the challenges he has faced and the lessons he has learned along the way. The bonds of brotherhood, the spirit of innovation, and the relentless pursuit of excellence have shaped him into the athlete he is today, ready to seize his moment of glory.

In a breathtaking final battle, Alex faces off against Achilles, the legendary hero whose name has become synonymous with invincibility. The virtual arena transforms into a grand coliseum, a fitting stage for the epic confrontation. The battle is a spectacle of skill and strategy, with each combatant pushing themselves to the limit. In the end, it is Alex's ingenuity and determination that prevail, securing his place as the Digital Champion and etching his name into the annals of history.

9

Chapter 9: The Aftermath of Victory

With the title of Digital Champion secured, Alex stands at the pinnacle of the Digital Colosseum. His journey has been one of relentless dedication, innovation, and perseverance, and his hard-earned victory is a testament to the indomitable spirit of competition. As the virtual confetti falls and the crowd roars in approval, Alex takes a moment to reflect on the path that brought him here.

The aftermath of victory is a whirlwind of celebrations and accolades. Alex becomes an instant celebrity, his name and achievements spreading like wildfire across the digital and real worlds. He is invited to interviews, featured in documentaries, and celebrated as a trailblazer in the new era of digital sports. The recognition is gratifying, but Alex remains grounded, knowing that his journey is far from over.

Amidst the celebrations, Alex is reminded of the bonds he formed with his fellow athletes. The friendships and camaraderie that developed over the course of the tournament become even more meaningful in the wake of his victory. Alex and his friends continue to support and uplift one another, celebrating each other's successes and sharing the joy of their collective achievements. The Digital Colosseum has forged a community of like-minded individuals, united by their passion for competition and the pursuit of excellence.

As the dust settles and the initial excitement wanes, Alex begins to contemplate his next steps. The world of digital sports is still evolving, and new challenges and opportunities lie ahead. Alex's victory in the Digital Colosseum is just the beginning, a stepping stone to even greater heights. With the support of his friends and the lessons he has learned, Alex is ready to embark on the next chapter of his journey, determined to continue pushing the boundaries of what is possible.

10

Chapter 10: Legends Reborn

The success of the Digital Colosseum marks the beginning of a new era in sports and entertainment, where the lines between myth and reality blur in spectacular fashion. The AI-controlled mythological heroes, brought to life by Athlon, capture the imagination of fans around the world. The stories of Achilles, Hercules, Athena, and other legendary figures are revitalized, their legends reborn in the digital age.

The impact of the Digital Colosseum extends beyond the virtual arena, inspiring a renewed interest in mythology and ancient legends. Scholars, artists, and creators draw inspiration from the stories of old, reimagining them in new and innovative ways. The fusion of technology and mythology creates a rich tapestry of narratives, where the past and the future converge in a celebration of human ingenuity and creativity.

The athletes who competed in the Digital Colosseum become modern-day legends in their own right, their names etched into the annals of history alongside the mythological heroes they faced. Their achievements serve as a beacon of inspiration, encouraging others to dream big and pursue their passions with unwavering determination. The Digital Colosseum becomes a symbol of the limitless potential of human creativity and the transformative power of technology.

As the world embraces this new era, the legacy of the Digital Colosseum continues to grow. New tournaments are organized, each one more ambitious and innovative than the last. The AI Engine, Athlon, evolves and adapts, creating ever more thrilling and dynamic challenges for the athletes. The spirit of competition and the allure of myth remain as strong as ever, driving the Digital Colosseum to new heights and ensuring that its legends will endure for generations to come.

11

Chapter 11: The Evolution of Athlon

As the years pass, the AI Engine, Athlon, continues to evolve and adapt, becoming ever more sophisticated and versatile. The team's dedication to innovation ensures that the AI remains at the cutting edge of technology, capable of generating increasingly complex and immersive scenarios. Athlon's growth is a testament to the power of human ingenuity, a reflection of the limitless potential of artificial intelligence when harnessed for creative and constructive purposes.

Dr. Elena Carter and her team remain at the forefront of Athlon's development, constantly pushing the boundaries of what the AI can achieve. They introduce new mythological heroes, expand the repertoire of challenges, and refine the algorithms that govern the virtual arenas. The athletes who compete in the Digital Colosseum benefit from these advancements, facing ever more thrilling and dynamic tests of their skill and determination.

The impact of Athlon extends beyond the world of sports, influencing fields as diverse as education, entertainment, and scientific research. The AI's ability to simulate complex scenarios and generate realistic environments finds applications in a wide range of industries, driving progress and innovation on a global scale. Athlon becomes a symbol of the transformative power of technology, inspiring a new generation of thinkers and creators to explore the possibilities of artificial intelligence.

As the Digital Colosseum continues to captivate audiences around the world, the legacy of Athlon and the heroes it brings to life endures. The AI's evolution is a testament to the power of collaboration and the pursuit of excellence, a reminder that the future is shaped by those who dare to dream big and push the boundaries of what is possible.

12

Chapter 12: A New Dawn

The Digital Colosseum stands as a monument to the power of human creativity and the limitless potential of technology. Its legacy is one of innovation, inspiration, and the relentless pursuit of excellence. As new generations of athletes step into the virtual arena, they carry forward the spirit of the pioneers who came before them, driven by the same passion and determination that defined the early days of the tournament.

Alex, now a mentor and coach, passes on the lessons he has learned to the next generation of competitors. He shares his knowledge and experiences, helping young athletes navigate the challenges of the Digital Colosseum and realize their full potential. The bonds of brotherhood that he formed during his own journey continue to inspire and uplift, fostering a sense of community and camaraderie that transcends the competition.

The mythological heroes who once graced the pages of ancient legends continue to captivate and inspire, their stories brought to life in the digital realm. The fusion of technology and mythology creates a rich and vibrant tapestry, where the past and the future intertwine in a celebration of human ingenuity and creativity. The Digital Colosseum becomes a living testament to the enduring power of stories, a reminder that the legends of old still have the power to inspire and transform.

As the sun sets on the Digital Colosseum, a new dawn rises, ushering in an era of endless possibilities. The athletes, heroes, and creators who inhabit this world stand at the forefront of a new frontier, ready to explore the uncharted territories of the digital age. The Digital Colosseum is more than just a virtual arena; it is a symbol of the boundless potential of human imagination and the transformative power of technology. The future is bright, and the adventure is just beginning.

13

Chapter 13: The Rise of New Legends

As new athletes step into the Digital Colosseum, they bring with them fresh perspectives and innovative approaches to the competition. The legacy of past champions, like Alex, serves as both an inspiration and a challenge, motivating the new generation to push the boundaries of what is possible. These rising stars are determined to make their mark, eager to carve out their own place in the annals of digital sports history.

Among these new contenders is Maya, a prodigious talent known for her lightning-fast reflexes and strategic brilliance. Her journey to the Digital Colosseum is marked by relentless training and an unwavering commitment to excellence. Maya quickly gains recognition for her unique blend of skill and ingenuity, capturing the attention of fans and competitors alike. As she navigates the challenges of the virtual arena, Maya's story becomes one of perseverance and innovation, embodying the spirit of the Digital Colosseum.

The new legends emerging in the Digital Colosseum reflect the evolving nature of the competition, as athletes adapt to the ever-changing landscape and leverage the latest advancements in technology. The virtual arenas continue to serve as a testing ground for human potential, where the fusion of myth and reality creates a rich tapestry of narratives. The rise of new legends ensures that the legacy of the Digital Colosseum remains vibrant and dynamic, inspiring future generations to dream big and reach for greatness.

Maya's journey is one of many, as athletes from diverse backgrounds and cultures come together to compete in the Digital Colosseum. Their stories intertwine, creating a rich mosaic of experiences and achievements. The bonds of brotherhood and the spirit of innovation remain at the heart of the competition, driving the athletes to push the boundaries of what is possible and achieve feats that will be remembered for generations to come.

14

Chapter 14: The Global Impact

The success of the Digital Colosseum has a profound impact on the world, reshaping the landscape of sports and entertainment. The virtual arenas become a global phenomenon, attracting audiences from every corner of the globe. Fans from diverse cultures and backgrounds come together to celebrate the spirit of competition and the timeless allure of mythological heroes. The Digital Colosseum becomes a symbol of unity and inclusivity, transcending borders and fostering a sense of global community.

The influence of the Digital Colosseum extends beyond the realm of sports, inspiring advancements in technology, education, and the arts. The AI Engine, Athlon, becomes a catalyst for innovation, driving progress in fields as diverse as virtual reality, artificial intelligence, and immersive storytelling. The fusion of technology and mythology creates new opportunities for creative expression, encouraging artists, writers, and creators to explore the possibilities of the digital age.

Educational institutions around the world embrace the potential of the Digital Colosseum, integrating its lessons and experiences into their curricula. Students are encouraged to think critically, innovate, and explore the intersections of technology and culture. The Digital Colosseum becomes a powerful tool for fostering creativity and curiosity, inspiring the next generation of thinkers and leaders to dream big and push the boundaries of what is possible.

THE DIGITAL COLOSSEUM, WHERE SPORTS, AI, AND MYTHOLOGICAL HEROES COLLIDE

The global impact of the Digital Colosseum is a testament to the power of human ingenuity and the transformative potential of technology. As the world continues to evolve, the legacy of the Digital Colosseum endures, inspiring new generations to embrace the spirit of competition, innovation, and unity. The Digital Colosseum stands as a beacon of hope and possibility, a reminder that the future is shaped by those who dare to dream and strive for greatness.

15

Chapter 15: The Future Awaits

As the Digital Colosseum continues to evolve, the possibilities for the future are limitless. The athletes, mythological heroes, and creators who inhabit this world are poised to explore new frontiers, pushing the boundaries of what is possible and redefining the landscape of sports and entertainment. The journey of the Digital Colosseum is far from over, with new challenges, innovations, and stories waiting to be discovered.

The AI Engine, Athlon, continues to grow and adapt, constantly evolving to meet the demands of the ever-changing digital landscape. New mythological heroes are introduced, each bringing their own unique abilities and stories to the virtual arena. The challenges become more complex and dynamic, ensuring that the competition remains thrilling and unpredictable. The Digital Colosseum becomes a living, breathing entity, a testament to the power of human creativity and the endless potential of technology.

The athletes who compete in the Digital Colosseum remain at the forefront of this exciting journey, their achievements and stories inspiring future generations to dream big and reach for greatness. The bonds of brotherhood, the spirit of innovation, and the pursuit of excellence continue to define the competition, driving the athletes to push themselves to new heights. The Digital Colosseum becomes a beacon of hope and possibility, a reminder that the future is shaped by those who dare to dream and strive for greatness.

As the sun sets on the Digital Colosseum and a new dawn rises, the world stands on the cusp of an exciting new era. The fusion of technology and mythology creates a rich tapestry of experiences and narratives, where the past and the future converge in a celebration of human ingenuity and creativity. The journey of the Digital Colosseum is just beginning, and the future awaits with endless possibilities.

The Digital Colosseum: Where Sports, AI, and Mythological Heroes Collide

Step into a world where the boundaries between myth and reality blur, and the spirit of competition reaches unprecedented heights. In this thrilling tale, "The Digital Colosseum" invites you to witness the ultimate fusion of sports, artificial intelligence, and ancient legends.

The story begins in a future where traditional stadiums have given way to virtual arenas, and athletes from around the globe compete in the awe-inspiring Digital Colosseum. Governed by the powerful AI Engine, Athlon, this virtual coliseum brings legendary heroes like Achilles, Hercules, and Athena to life, creating a spectacle that captivates audiences worldwide.

Follow the journey of Alex, a rising star in the world of digital sports, as he navigates the challenges and trials of the Digital Colosseum. Alongside his fellow competitors, Alex must face both human rivals and AI-controlled mythological heroes, pushing the limits of skill and determination. As the competition intensifies, the athletes form deep bonds of camaraderie, united by their shared experiences and the pursuit of excellence.

Under the visionary leadership of Dr. Elena Carter and her team, Athlon continues to evolve, driving innovation and transforming the landscape of sports and entertainment. The Digital Colosseum becomes a global phenomenon, inspiring new generations to embrace the possibilities of technology and the timeless allure of myth.

"The Digital Colosseum" is a celebration of human ingenuity, creativity, and the indomitable spirit of competition. Join Alex and a cast of unforgettable characters as they embark on a journey of discovery, innovation, and triumph in a world where sports, AI, and mythological heroes collide.

www.ingramcontent.com/pod-product-compliance
Lightning Source LLC
LaVergne TN
LVHW020502080526
838202LV00057B/6120